Angela Gray's
Cookery School
Spring Recipes
Photographs Huw Jones

Spring Recipes
Angela Gray's Cookery School
Published in Great Britain in 2019 by
Graffeg Limited.

Graffeg Limited, 24 Stradey Park Business
Centre, Mwrwg Road, Llangennech,
Llanelli, Carmarthenshire SA14 8YP Wales
UK Tel 01554 824000 www.graffeg.com

A CIP Catalogue record for this book is
available from the British Library.

ISBN 9781912213337

1 2 3 4 5 6 7 8 9

Photo credits

Angela Gray's

Cookery School

Spring Recipes

Photographs Huw Jones

GRAFFEG

Contents

Desserts

The Welsh Collection

Introduction

Spring is in the air!

No matter how challenging the winter months have been, how soggy the ground has become, how bare the trees look against gloomy skies, and how dismal those days can seem – nature just never fails to shake it all off and push forward.

The spring morning light is beautifully bright, highlighting all the new that is happening in nature. Fresh life emerges all around us, in our gardens, parklands and the countryside, with the first flowers of the season popping up to delight. In the early hours, dawn breaks accompanied by the sound of bird song and the sunlight strikes through our drawn curtains, urging us to rise and seize the day.

It's quite apt that I end my series of seasonal cookery books with spring, as it represents so many possibilities. The chance of starting a new adventure, growing an idea and feeling that a new chapter is unfolding; it's all part of the constant renewal and continuous, ever-changing cycle of wonder that is life.

This is also reflected in what I cook and eat. After the months of winter warmers, one-pot wonders and rich roasts, I start to yearn for a fresher and lighter approach to cooking. This is also accompanied by the need for a big spring clean of my home!

The kitchen is important as I spend a lot of my time there. I love pots of herbs on my windowsill and I always have a vase of daffodils on the table from the first moment they become available. A lovely candle with the aroma of citrus and herbs

completes the spring makeover of my surroundings and sets the scene for some new culinary ideas to emerge.

Bringing the first shop of new season ingredients into the kitchen is still exciting for me. There is always a new idea to try, bringing a freshness and vigour to everyday cooking. I love all the green vegetables that are available, some of which only have a short season, such as asparagus, spring greens and purple sprouting broccoli.

I have used some of these to make delicious salads, such as 'Green

Day!' and 'Yellow Cauliflower', and both demonstrate some different ways of bringing good flavours and textures together.

I could have dedicated the whole book to my love of asparagus. I love the fat bundles of spears we get from the Wye Valley Producers, the quality is excellent and such a treat; you almost feel like you have picked them yourself. When you have something so ripe and ready, just the simplest execution is needed in cooking. It's all about making the most of everything in the moment and I just love that. My recipe for asparagus with butter sauce echoes this and is often on the menu throughout the season.

Growing up on a farm, we didn't have asparagus in the vegetable garden, but we did have a plentiful supply of seasonal ingredients to feed a busy and hungry family. Spring was a busy time on the farm and demanding in terms of round the clock monitoring during the lambing season. I remember it being uncharacteristically quiet in the house, everyone too bleary eyed to make conversation. This momentary hardship was always softened with having good food to keep you energised and spirits lifted. A firm favourite during this busy time would be a home cooked gammon. We would enjoy it simply with a traditional parsley sauce. The next day, some shredded leftover gammon was delicious in a cheesy pasta bake. Beyond that for supper, sandwiches were delivered with a fresh flask of tea to the lambing shed, offering a little welcomed comfort for those on the graveyard shift.

I have included my recipe for a lovely Gammon and Parsley Sauce and offer Candied New Potatoes, which I discovered when staying with my family in Canada. I later found out that this recipe was based on a traditional Danish dish called "Browned Potatoes" which were enjoyed by my mum and her brothers when they stayed in

Denmark. It always amazes me how recipes can travel and morph into something else.

Looking back, the way my mum cooked became the starting point of me growing my own ideas in developing recipes. For instance, the first new season lamb of the year served for a family gathering at Easter, with our home-grown new potatoes, baby carrots and purple sprouting; has become Stuffed Shoulder of Welsh Lamb with Farro, Capers and Lemon. A Mediterranean take on that family favourite cultured from my days growing up on the farm and later, working as a chef in the Mediterranean.

From family tradition and travels afar to wonderful memories, it all forms part of the very special time I have had putting these books together. I finish with a memory of sitting with my lovely mum in the spring of 2013, she was reaching the last stages of her illness and wanted to get things in order. Part of that was choosing the music and the menu for her life celebration. We were so in awe of her, she wanted to look after friends and family and for us all to have a party!

One request that really stands out for me was for Queen of Puddings. This was a treat she made when I was very young, and times were frugal. Stale bread, soaked in beaten egg yolk, a little milk and sugar, baked until set then topped with jam and a hand whisked meringue. Then baked again until golden – it was so wonderful, just like magic to a child.

For her wake, the dessert was made in mini tartlets with majestic little crowns of meringue. In the dessert section of this book, I have elevated her favourite dessert to heavenly heights, using a brioche base, topped with a twist of lemon and elderflower, followed by a golden whippy Swiss meringue top. I think she would approve.

Angela Gray

Wild Garlic and Nettle Soup

Ingredients

100g fresh leaf spinach, rinsed well and drained

75g butter

1 medium onion, peeled and finely diced

450g potatoes, peeled and diced

200g wild garlic leaves, rinsed well and drained

200g young nettle leaves and tender stalks, rinsed well and drained. Handle with gloves!

800ml chicken or vegetable stock

600ml whole milk

200ml crème fraîche

¼ teaspoon fresh grated nutmeg

Freshly ground pepper and sea salt to season

Serves 4-6

What you do

1. Melt the butter in a large pan over a low heat, add the onion and potato, stir through and place a sheet of foil or baking parchment directly on top. Place a lid on the pan and cook for 15 minutes. Halfway through remove the lid and foil/paper, stir the potato and onion, add a ladle of stock and then replace the foil/paper and lid. Continue cooking until the vegetables are soft through, but not browned.

2. Remove the lid and foil/parchment, pour in the remaining stock and the milk, cover and simmer gently for 20 minutes.

3. Remove the lid and add the wild garlic leaves (retaining a few for garnish), nettles and spinach. Return the lid and simmer gently for 10 minutes.

4. Allow to cool a little and then use a stick blender to liquidise the soup until smooth. Taste the flavour

and add the freshly-ground nutmeg, black pepper and sea salt as needed.

Return to the heat and bring back to serving temperature, but do not allow to boil. Stir in the crème fraîche, shred the remaining garlic leaves, sprinkle in and serve.

If you don't have time to forage, add a large clove of grated garlic once the onions and potatoes are soft to give a subtle garlicky flavour. Then substitute the nettles with more spinach and a little rocket.

Mini Cheese Muffins

These little cheesy numbers are utterly delicious served warm with a good smear of butter.

Ingredients

25g butter

4 spring onions trimmed and finely chopped

150g self-raising flour

50g mature Cheddar cheese, finely grated

1 teaspoon mustard powder

1 teaspoon sea salt

½ teaspoon black pepper

¼ teaspoon cayenne pepper

1 large free-range egg

125ml whole milk

Makes 24

What you do

1. Preheat your oven to 180°C/160°C Fan/Gas 4 and line a 24-hole mini muffin tin with paper cases. Heat a frying pan over a low heat, melt the butter and fry the spring onion until just soft. Drain on some kitchen paper.

2. In a medium bowl, mix together the flour, three-quarters of the cheese, the mustard powder, salt, pepper and cayenne.

3. In a separate bowl, mix together the egg, milk and cooked onion. Add the wet ingredients to the bowl of dry ingredients and mix until just combined (do not over-mix, or the muffins will be tough).

4. Divide the mixture among the cases and sprinkle over the remaining cheese. Bake for 12 minutes or until golden and springy to the touch. Serve warm or at room temperature.

These can be made in advance and gently warmed before serving. You can also freeze them. Reheat the muffins in foil at 180°C/Fan 160°C/ Gas 4 for 15 minutes, 20 minutes if cooking from frozen. Open the foil and cook for a further 5 minutes to crisp up.

Little Cheese and Spring Herb Soufflés with Wild Garlic Velouté

Ingredients

Base Sauce

1 small onion, peeled and sliced

275ml whole milk

2 peppercorns

¼ teaspoon celery salt

1 bay leaf

40g unsalted butter – plus extra for buttering ramekins

40g plain flour

The rest of the ingredients

100g good mature Cheddar cheese

50g Parmesan, finely grated

25g breadcrumbs

50g soft goats' cheese e.g. Pantysgawn, or a soft Blue e.g. Perl Las

1 teaspoon English mustard powder

¼ teaspoon freshly grated nutmeg

1 level teaspoon sea salt

¼ teaspoon black pepper

¼ teaspoon cayenne pepper

3 free-range eggs, separated, plus 1 extra egg white

1 heaped tablespoon of chopped spring herbs e.g. parsley, chervil, chives

For the second baking

50ml dry white wine

200ml crème fraîche

100g wild garlic leaves, rinsed and drained

Sea salt and pepper to season

1 tablespoon wild garlic pesto (see page 52)

Makes 6

What you do

1 **To make the sauce base** – put the onion into a saucepan with the milk, peppercorns, celery salt and bay leaf. Bring to a gentle simmer over a low heat and cook for 5 minutes to infuse the flavours. Remove from the heat and set aside for a couple of minutes.

2 Melt the butter in a medium non-stick saucepan over a low heat. Remove from the heat and stir in the flour. Once combined, return to a low heat and cook for a minute, stirring as it begins to bubble, then remove from the heat.

3 Strain the milk through a sieve into a jug to remove the flavourings. You will need around 250ml of infused milk, so discard any excess or top up as needed with fresh milk.

4 Gradually stir the milk into the flour and butter paste, then return to the heat and cook for 2 minutes, bringing to the boil and stirring constantly. The sauce will become smooth and thick. Add the Cheddar cheese, mustard, nutmeg, salt, pepper and cayenne and continue to cook for a further 1-2 minutes more until the cheese melts. Stir in the herbs.

5 Transfer the cheese sauce to a bowl and leave to stand for 5 minutes. Once the mixture has cooled, beat in the egg yolks one at a time until thoroughly mixed.

6 Whisk the egg whites in a bowl until stiff peaks are formed when the whisk is removed. Fold in one heaped tablespoon of the egg whites into the cheese mixture and mix well. (This makes folding the remaining egg whites in easier). Then gently fold in the remaining egg whites to preserve the volume you have created.

7 **To cook the soufflés** – preheat the oven to 150°C/120°C Fan/Gas 3.

8 Generously butter 6 x 150ml ovenproof ramekins and line the bases with a disc of baking parchment. Mix half of the Parmesan with the breadcrumbs and use this to coat the inside of the ramekins, using any remaining mixture to sprinkle over the tops of the soufflés.

9 Place in a roasting tin lined with parchment. Spoon the soufflé mixture into the ramekins until it almost reaches the top. Divide the goats' or blue cheese into 6 portions and gently insert into each soufflé. Pour enough boiling water into the roasting tin to come one-third of the way up the ramekins. Sprinkle the remaining breadcrumbs and Parmesan over the top.

10 Bake in the centre of the oven for about 20 minutes until they have set, risen slightly and are pale in colour. Remove the ramekins carefully from the roasting tin and cool.

11 **To make the wild garlic velouté** – heat the wine and crème fraîche together in a small pan. Simmer for 5 minutes, then add the wild garlic and cook for 4 minutes until the leaves are soft. Blitz to a smooth sauce using a stick blender, season with sea salt and black pepper. Cover and cool. Pop in the fridge until needed.

12 When the soufflés are cold, line a baking tray with baking parchment and slide a knife around the edge of each ramekin. Carefully turn the soufflés out onto your hand. Remove the baking paper disc from the base.

13 Place on the tray upside down. The soufflés can now be covered with cling film and chilled for up to 24 hours before being baked again.

14 **For the second baking** – preheat the oven to 200°C/180°C Fan/Gas 6. Fifteen minutes before serving, remove the cling film from the

soufflés. Bake for 10-12 minutes until the soufflés are puffed and golden. Whilst they are cooking, gently re-heat the wild garlic velouté. Plate the soufflés, spoon the velouté over the top and finish with a teaspoon of pesto.

Grilled Wye Valley Asparagus with Butter Sauce and Herb Crumb

Seasonal ingredients at the
peak of readiness need only the
simplest touches in the kitchen.

Ingredients

24 thick asparagus spears

Butter sauce

200g unsalted butter

1 medium free-range egg, plus 1 egg yolk

2-3 tablespoons of lemon juice, depending on your taste

150ml very soft, whipped double cream

100g stale breadcrumbs – sourdough or focaccia are best

2 tablespoons olive oil

1 heaped tablespoon mixed spring herbs, chopped

Serves 4-6

What you do

1. **To make the butter sauce** – Cut the butter into small cubes and pop into a small saucepan and melt over a low heat. Place the egg, egg yolk, lemon juice and seasoning into the bowl of a small food processor (or you can do this by hand with a whisk if you have the energy!). Process or whisk the eggs and lemon juice until very thick and pale in colour – about 5 minutes (10 minutes by hand).

2. When the eggs have thickened, reheat the butter until it is just beginning to bubble and remove any scum from the surface with a spoon. Then, with the whisk or motor still running, slowly add the hot butter to the egg mixture until you see it begin to thicken. Only use the liquid butter, leave any milky residue behind. Tip the sauce into a bowl and keep it warm. I usually put it over a saucepan with some boiled water in it.

3 **To prepare the breadcrumbs** – mix the breadcrumbs with the olive oil. Heat a frying pan and fry the crumbs until toasted and crisp. Stir in the chopped herbs, cook for a further minute, then remove and drain on kitchen paper.

4 **To prepare the asparagus spears** – Snap the stem near the end to find the beginning of the softer part of the spear. Line them all up and cut them at that point. Peel the spears with a vegetable peeler to remove the cuticles. Heat a wide pan of water to boiling point and add 1 teaspoon of sea salt. Add the asparagus and cook for about 4-6 minutes or until tender through when pierced with the tip of a sharp knife. Drain well.

5 **To assemble** – Whisk the whipped cream into the hot butter sauce, taste and adjust the seasoning to your liking. Plate the asparagus, spoon half of the sauce over the top and finish with the breadcrumbs. Serve the remaining sauce at the table.

Asparagus can also be steamed for a few minutes until just tender, serve with a poached egg and a little bacon crumb to finish; or, try brushing them with a little olive oil and griddling them until just tender, serve with poached or steamed fish – delish.

Potted Seafood

Ingredients

200g salted butter

1 heaped teaspoon lemon zest, grated

2 tablespoons lemon juice – you may like a little more

½ teaspoon black pepper

¼ teaspoon of ground mace

½ teaspoon cayenne pepper

100g chunks of salmon or sea trout

150g cooked brown shrimp

150g cooked white crab meat

50g cooked brown crab meat

1 tablespoon herbs, chopped – I use parsley, chives, fennel and chervil

Serves 6

What you do

1. Gently melt the butter in a large frying pan, add the lemon zest, lemon juice, black pepper, mace, cayenne, chunks of salmon or sea trout and poach gently for 5 minutes, mashing the cubes of fish with the back of a spoon as it cooks.

2. When almost cooked, add the shrimp and both crab meats. Fold in and continue cooking until heated through. If you have a digital thermometer, the mixture should be 65°C. Remove from the heat and fold in the herbs.

3. Spoon and press the mixture into 6 ramekins, or a 500g clip jar. I like to layer the seafood with pickled cucumber or samphire and serve with crusty soda bread. Delish!

Pickled samphire or cucumber

1. Gently peel and deseed 1 cucumber and slice thinly into long strips – a vegetable peeler makes easy work of this.

2. If using samphire, blanch 150g for 1 minute in boiling water, then refresh in cold water.

3. Mix 4 tablespoons of white wine vinegar with a teaspoon of sugar, add pepper and a heaped teaspoon of chopped chives, dill or fennel.

4. Add the cucumber or samphire, mix well and cover. Leave for at least 30 minutes to marinade.

5. Keep in the fridge before serving.

It is important to remove the potted seafood from the fridge about 40 minutes before serving so that the flavours come alive. Hot toast or good crusty bread is all you need to serve with this, along with a glass of chilled white wine!

Baked Sea Trout with Potato and Sorrel Gratin

Ingredients

1 filleted sewin/sea trout, or a piece of salmon fillet 1.0kg -1.5kg

Brine

5L luke warm water

2 tablespoons sea salt

1 teaspoon sugar

1 garlic clove, sliced

½ medium lemon, sliced

A few parsley stalks

4 black peppercorns

Rub

1 heaped teaspoon sea salt

1 flat teaspoon black pepper corns, crushed

1 flat teaspoon pink peppercorns, crushed

1 dessertspoon fennel seeds, crushed

½ teaspoon sugar

1 teaspoon garlic granules

Zest of 1 medium lemon

Filling

1 unwaxed lemon, thinly sliced and blanched in salted water for 2 minutes

1 small bunch of spring herbs – parsley, chives, chervil, soft-stem thyme

100g butter

Serves 6

What you do

1. First, brine the fish for 45 minutes to 1 hour. Place all the ingredients into a large bowl, along with the 5 litres of lukewarm water, mix to dissolve the salt and sugar. Add the fish, cover with cling film and set aside.

2. Prepare the rub by placing everything, apart from the lemon zest, into a pestle and mortar and pound together until aromatic. Stir in the lemon zest.

Prepare the filling by making sure the lemon slices are sliced thinly and the herb leaves are picked and roughly chopped.

3 **To assemble** – Drain the fish well and pat dry. If using a large side of salmon, cut it in half, tucking the tail under slightly to create two even halves. Apply the rub all over the fish. Lay one half on a roasting tin lined with parchment paper. Dot with half of the butter, then a layer of half of the lemon slices and the herbs. Top with the remaining fillet, dot with butter and arrange the rest of the lemon slices along the centre of the fillet. I secure the fillets together with string in 5 places along the length, tying on top and trimming excess string.

4 **To cook** – Bake in a preheated oven at 200°C/180°C Fan/Gas 6 for 30 minutes. Remove, cover loosely with foil and rest for 10 minutes. Snip away the string and baste with the juices. Serve in thick slices with the potato and sorrel gratin.

This is such an impressive supper dish and you can make it all the day before. You then have it ready to cook on the day, leaving you plenty of time to relax with friends. I serve this with seasonal steamed asparagus, the perfect partner for fish.

Potato and Sorrel Gratin

Ingredients

6 medium potatoes, Maris Piper are great, peeled, thinly sliced, rinsed and drained

1 medium onion, finely sliced

200g sorrel leaf or spinach, mixed with 1 tablespoon of lemon juice

2 teaspoons Dijon or wholegrain mustard

250ml double cream

75ml whole milk

100g good Cheddar or Gruyère cheese

Sea salt and pepper to taste

Melted butter for brushing

Serves 4-6

What you do

1. Preheat the oven to 200°C/180°C Fan/Gas 6.

2. Brush a gratin dish lightly with melted butter and arrange a layer of potato over the base, slightly overlapping. Season with a little sprinkle of salt and pepper and continue to season as you add the layers. Top with one third of the onion. Repeat this process again, then add a layer of the sorrel or spinach, topping with another two layers of onion and then potato.

3. In a bowl, combine the cream, milk and mustard and mix together.

4. Pour over the potato mixture. Cover the dish with foil.

6 Place in the oven on a baking sheet and bake for 30 minutes then remove the foil and bake for a further 30 minutes. Remove the dish and top with the grated cheese, return to the oven and bake for a final 20 minutes. The potato should be deliciously soft throughout and golden on top.

Sorrel is such an easy plant to grow and I urge you to invest in a couple of pots. I have some large pots of it in my garden and it returns every year, showing off its long, deep-green leaves, ready for me to use in a few key seasonal dishes. Like most ingredients, I treasure and use it whilst I can.

Fish Tagine

This is such a deliciously delicate and aromatic dish. The perfect way to cook and enjoy fish.

Ingredients

For the marinade

2 teaspoons ground cumin

1 teaspoon ground coriander

1 teaspoon lemon zest

4 tablespoons lemon juice

2 large garlic cloves, finely grated

1 mild green chilli, finely chopped

1 small bunch fresh coriander, chopped

1 teaspoon sea salt

The rest

4 x 150g white fish fillets e.g. hake, pollock, cod, monk

500g waxy new potatoes, peeled and quartered

4 garlic cloves, finely grated

3 tablespoons olive oil

300g spring carrot, scrubbed and sliced

250g tinned, chopped tomatoes

100ml fish or vegetable stock

100g large pitted green olives

150g cooked cockles (optional)

100g white crab meat (optional)

To serve

6 Lemon wedges and 1 tablespoon fresh chopped coriander

Serves 4

What you do

1. **First, make the marinade** – Place all the ingredients in a mini processor or a pestle and mortar. Whiz/pound to combine to a smooth paste. Rub half over the fish fillets, cover and chill for an hour.

2. Meanwhile, boil the potatoes in a pan of salted water until tender, about 15-20 minutes.

3. In a shallow casserole or large pan over a low heat, fry the garlic

in the oil for 1-2 minutes. Add the carrots and cook for 5 minutes, then add the chopped tomatoes and cook for a further 2 minutes. Stir in the remaining marinade and the fish/ vegetable stock. Season well.

4 Preheat your oven to 200°C/180°C Fan/Gas 6. Place the potatoes in a tagine or a large casserole pan with a lid. Top with half the tomato mixture, then with the fish, then add the remaining tomato mixture. Scatter over the olives, cover and cook in the oven for 20 minutes, remove the lid and add the cockles and crab, cover with the lid and cook for another 8-10 minutes until the fish is just cooked through. Remove the tagine/ casserole and leave to stand for 5 minutes. Garnish with lemon wedges and chopped coriander.

I have included two very different salad recipes in this book; both make great company for this dish. If you are eating light, a good portion of either the 'Green Day' or 'Yellow Cauliflower' dishes are brilliant. Both are full of goodness and flavour.

Classic Pea and Asparagus Risotto with Three Toppings

This recipe takes the humble risotto to a whole new level!

Ingredients

Risotto

30g butter

1 tablespoon extra-virgin olive oil

1 small onion, peeled and finely chopped

350g arborio rice

125ml dry white wine

1.2L vegetable or chicken stock

1 courgette, cut into small cubes

8 asparagus stems, trimmed and finely chopped

100g petit pois

30g parmesan, grated

Topping 1: Parmesan crisp

60g coarsely grated Parmesan

¼ teaspoon black pepper

6 slices of Parma ham

Topping 2: The sauce

100ml stock

50ml white wine

1 heaped tablespoon crème fraîche

50g spinach or wild garlic

Serves 4

What you do

1 **First, make the garnishes** – To make the Parmesan crisps, place 8 small mounds of cheese on a baking sheet lined with parchment paper brushed with a little oil.

2 For the Parma ham, lay the slices on a baking sheet lined with foil brushed lightly with oil. Place a sheet of foil on top and weigh down with another baking sheet.

3 Bake both the Parmesan crisps and Parma ham at 180°C/160°C Fan/Gas 4 until crisp and golden, about 15 minutes.

4 **To make the risotto** – Pour the stock into a saucepan, bring it to the boil, then reduce the heat to low and leave it gently simmering.

5 Heat the extra virgin olive oil in a heavy-based saucepan, add the butter and then the onion and sauté over a medium heat until softened but not coloured. Stir in the rice with a wooden spoon and mix well to coat the grains.

6 Add the wine and allow to evaporate, stirring all the time, and then add a couple of ladles of hot stock, stirring continuously until the stock is absorbed.

7 Add more stock and repeat. Continue adding stock, cooking and stirring in this way for about 20 minutes, until the rice is almost cooked. Add the vegetables and stir through to combine, add a little more stock and cook until the vegetables are cooked.

8 Remove from the heat and stir in the Parmesan. Leave to rest for one minute.

9 **To make the sauce** – warm the stock and wine together, add the spinach or wild garlic and the crème fraîche. Bring to the boil and remove from the heat and blitz to a puree using a stick blender.

10 **To assemble** – ladle the risotto into warmed bowls, pour the sauce over the top and stud the centre with the Parmesan crisps and Parma ham – serve.

Note – At first glance this recipe may look a little involved, but the additional elements can all be made in advance and gently warmed through before serving. The risotto can also be part-cooked in advance, just like they do in restaurants, making life a lot easier. Just take the risotto in point 7 to 10 minutes cooking, instead of 20 minutes. Remove and cool, keeping in the fridge until needed. When ready, resume the cooking from that point, i.e. 10 more minutes, adding the stock and then the vegetables etc.

Classic White Chicken Stock

Ingredients

1.5kg chicken bones – cooked carcasses can be used

1 medium onion

1 stick celery

1 medium carrot

1 bay leaf

5 parsley stems

4 black peppercorns

1 clove

4 sprigs thyme

Makes approximately 1.5L

What you do

The neck, back, ribs and wings are excellent for making chicken stock.

When making the stock, always start with cold water. This helps extract more collagen, giving the stock more body. When cooking the stock, simmer gently rather than boil. Stirring is not necessary, just skim away any scum that forms on the surface and top up the water level if it falls below the bones.

1. Place the bay leaf, parsley, peppercorns, clove and thyme into a piece of muslin and tie into a bag for your bouquet garni.

2. Rinse the chicken bones in cold water and transfer to a heavy-bottomed saucepan.

3. Add enough cold water to the pot to completely cover the bones.

4. Bring the pot to a boil, then immediately drain and rinse the bones.

5. Return the bones to the pot and cover with fresh, cold water.

6. Bring to the boil, then lower the heat until it simmers. Skim away any scum that rises to the surface.

7. Finely chop all the vegetables to create a mirepoix and add this to the pan together with the bouquet garni.

8. Simmer for about 4 hours, continuing to skim the impurities that rise to the surface. Liquid will evaporate, so make sure there is always enough water to cover the bones.

9. After 4 hours, remove from the heat and strain the stock through a sieve lined with a few layers of cheesecloth. Cool the stock completely, and then refrigerate or freeze.

Chicken stock is incredibly versatile. You can use it as a base for soups and sauces, as cooking liquid for rice or risotto, or for braising poultry or vegetables.

Handmade Ravioli filled with Goats' Cheese and Wild Garlic

Ingredients

400g '00' pasta flour plus extra for rolling out

1 level teaspoon salt

3 large eggs + 1 egg yolk

Filling

250g soft goats' cheese – Pantysgawn is delicious

1 tablespoon spring herbs, chopped – parsley, chives, thyme

1 tablespoon toasted pine nuts

1 rounded teaspoon of grated lemon zest

¼ teaspoon grated nutmeg

2 heaped tablespoons soft, sticky, cooked onion (sauté 1 medium finely -chopped onion in 2 tablespoons of olive oil slowly until soft, sticky and slightly coloured, about 15 minutes)

150g blanched and well drained wild garlic or spinach, chopped

40g Parmesan cheese

Wild garlic pesto

150g wild garlic, blanched and drained

1 teaspoon sea salt

¼ teaspoon black pepper

50g pine nuts or blanched almonds

100ml olive oil

75g Parmesan, grated

Serves 4-6

What you do

1. **To make the pesto** – Place all the ingredients in a blender and pulse to combine into a smooth paste. Taste and adjust the seasoning to your taste. If the paste is a little thick, loosen slightly with a little olive oil. Cover and set aside until needed.

2. **To make the pasta dough** – Tip the flour into a pile on your work surface, add the sea salt and mix together, making a large crater in the middle. Break in the eggs

and egg yolk and gradually mix in the flour. Before forcing the whole mixture together, check it's not too dry. You can flick a little cold water over the surface and then push everything together into a soft dough ball.

3 **Now to work the dough** – Begin by gently folding the dough onto itself, flattening, and folding again. It will be soft at first, then gradually start to firm up. Once it's firm enough to knead, begin kneading the dough. Incorporate more flour as needed to prevent the dough from sticking to you or the work surface. The dough is ready when it forms a smooth elastic ball and has very few air bubbles when cut.

4 Place the dough onto a sheet of cling film and wrap, setting aside for 30 minutes.

5 **Next, make the filling** – Mix together the cheese, chopped herbs, roasted pine nuts, lemon zest, grated nutmeg, cooked onion, chopped wild garlic or spinach and Parmesan cheese. Taste and add sea salt and black pepper to your taste.

Now you are ready to roll! The name of the game at this point is to keep everything well-floured to prevent the pasta from sticking to itself or the roller as you work. If the dough starts to feel sticky as you roll it, sprinkle it with flour. Also sprinkle flour on any pasta you're not working with (rolled, cut or otherwise) and keep it covered with a clean tea-towel.

6 Cut the dough into 4 portions and place 3 under the cloth. Set your pasta machine to the thickest setting (usually marked "1"). Flatten the one piece of dough into a thick disk between your hands and feed it through the pasta roller. Repeat twice. Fold this piece of dough into thirds, like folding a letter, and press it between your hands again. With the pasta machine still on

the widest setting, feed the pasta crosswise between the rollers. Feed it through once or twice more until smooth.

7 Begin changing the settings on your roller to roll the pasta thinner and thinner, rolling the pasta twice on each setting. If the sheet of pasta gets too long to manage, lay it on a cutting board and slice it in half. Roll the pasta to setting 7.

8 Lay the sheet on a floured surface, cut out circles with a cutter or a ravioli cutter and place under a tea towel. Lay out 8 pasta circles, wet the edges, spoon ½ teaspoon of filling in the centre, top with another pasta circle and seal the edges – place on a floured tray. Repeat until all the pasta is used up.

9 Cook the pasta in a large pan of salted water for 3-4 minutes, drain well, tip into a serving dish or onto plates and drizzle with the pesto.

Note: You can roll the pasta by hand – use a little flour on the surface, flatten one piece of dough at a time and roll out. Put your weight behind the heels of your hands and make short, sharp rolls forward with the rolling pin, stretching the dough forward. It will spring back, but persevere, adding a little flour only when needed. Cut and fill as in the recipe above.

You can open freeze the ravioli and then pop into a freezer bag to store easily. Cook in salted boiling water from frozen for 4 minutes.

In addition, you can roll up and shred the off cuts by hand and cook in salted boiling water for 3 minutes, drain and serve with some pesto as a lunch treat!

Green Day!

Simple, clean and green!

Ingredients

Salad

300g long-stem purple sprouting or broccoli, trimmed

150g defrosted peas

1 Little Gem lettuce or similar

2 spring onions, finely sliced

1 large handful rocket leaves

250g buffalo mozzarella or burrata

Dressing

1 teaspoon Dijon mustard

1 large garlic clove, chopped and pasted with ½ teaspoon of sea salt

1 tablespoon white wine vinegar

2 tablespoons extra-virgin olive or rapeseed oil

¼ teaspoon sugar

4 stems each of mint and parsley leaves

Serves 4

What you do

1. First cook the broccoli or purple sprouting – use a steamer over a pan of simmering water or cook directly in boiling water. Cook for 3-5 minutes until the stems are tender when pierced with a knife.

2. Add the peas when the broccoli is almost cooked, they need just a minute. Drain the vegetables and place in a bowl of ice-cold water to refresh and cool. Drain and pat dry with kitchen paper.

3. **Make the dressing** – Add everything into a bowl and whisk together, then stir in the spring onions.

4. **To serve** –Spread the lettuce leaves over a platter or between 4 plates. Scatter with the broccoli and peas and tear the mozzarella or burrata and dot over the greens. Spoon the dressing over the top and top with rocket leaves and the torn leaves of mint and parsley.

Sometimes I just love a good salad bowl, especially if I feel I have been over indulging a little! The ingredients are versatile; I sometimes swap the mozzarella or burrata for some succulent chopped roast chicken and crisp pancetta, making a delicious addition to the vegetables for a fabulous lunch. It is equally lovely served as a simple salad without any cheese or meat and makes the perfect accompaniment for some grilled fish or meat.

Yellow Cauliflower

Who thought we would be so in love with cauliflower!

Ingredients

1 large cauliflower, cut into medium slices

1 medium onion, peeled, halved and cut into medium slices

Sea salt and black pepper for seasoning

Dressing

1 rounded teaspoon turmeric powder

4 tablespoons lemon juice

1 tablespoon rapeseed or sunflower oil

1 tablespoon honey

To finish

1 small bunch of herbs such as chives, parsley and mint, chopped

50g dried chopped mango

1 tablespoon sherry vinegar

1 teaspoon honey

Serves 4-6

What you do

1. Cut the larger slices of cauliflower in half and place on a large baking tray or roasting tin lined with baking parchment. Put the slices of onion between the cauliflower pieces. Sprinkle with sea salt and black pepper.

2. Mix the dressing by whisking everything together and then brush over the cauliflower and onion. Roast in a preheated oven at 180°C/160°C Fan/Gas 4, until lightly golden at the edges – about 40 minutes.

3. To finish, spoon the cauliflower and onions into a dish, finish with the chopped herbs and dried mango, drizzle with the sherry vinegar and honey.

I love to make this into a delicious lunch bowl by adding a few other ingredients. Take one tablespoon of plump dried fruit, such as sour cherries, sultanas or mango (soak in water for 20 minutes), a dessertspoon of toasted flaked almonds, or another nut you like, then add a handful of shredded spinach leaves or some rocket and 50g of crumbled feta, or cubes of blue cheese. Mix together and pop in a container to eat later.

Gammon with
Parsley Sauce and
Candied Potatoes

Ingredients

2kg piece of gammon, soaked in water overnight

1 large onion, peeled and halved, each studded with 4 cloves

12 peppercorns

2 bay leaves

1 large leek, washed and shredded

2 large carrots, peeled and sliced

4 sticks of celery, plus leaves, chopped

2L apple juice

Water to top up

Parsley Sauce

1.5L full fat milk

1 small onion studded with 4 cloves

Bay leaf

5 black peppercorns

130g butter

130g plain flour

1 dessertspoon Dijon mustard

¼ teaspoon chilli powder

100ml crème fraîche

100g parsley leaves, chopped

Sea salt and black pepper to taste

Candied Potatoes

450g small new potatoes, scraped and cooked

25g butter

1 large garlic glove, peeled and grated

3 tablespoons runny honey

1 teaspoon lemon zest

2 tablespoons lemon juice

Salt and pepper to taste

1 tablespoon chopped chives or spring onion to finish

Serves 8-10

What you do

Note: Always check when you buy your gammon whether it needs soaking, as sometimes the meat can be a little too salty; I always soak mine as a precaution and I find the result better. To be sure, you can do what my Nain always did: pop it into a large pan and cover with water, bring it to the boil for 5 minutes, drain and then continue as in the recipe.

1 Drain the gammon and place in a large saucepan. Add all the vegetables, flavourings, apple juice and enough water to cover the meat. Place over a medium to high heat and bring to the boil. Reduce the heat down to a slow simmer and, using a slotted spoon, skim away any of the white foam from the surface. Cover with a lid or sheet of foil and cook gently for 2 hours, checking occasionally in case the liquid level needs topping up.

2 The gammon should be really soft at the end of the cooking time, insert a small knife and it should go in easily. If you are cooking the gammon the day before you plan to serve it, then leave it to cool in the liquid. This will keep it deliciously moist. If using the same day, remove the gammon from the liquid onto a warm plate, loosely cover with foil and rest for 20 minutes whilst you make the sauce and the potatoes.

3 **To make the sauce** – Pour the milk into a pan, add the clove-studded onion, bay leaf and peppercorns and bring up to the boil, then turn off the heat and leave to cool and let the flavours infuse. When ready, strain the milk into a jug. Melt the butter in a saucepan, stir in the flour and cook gently for 1 minute over the heat. Stir in the mustard and chilli powder, remove from the heat and slowly pour in the milk a little at a time so that the paste is loosened evenly and lump free. Once all the milk is combined,

return to the heat and stir until thickened, boiling it gently and briefly for 2 minutes.

4 Reduce the heat and stir in the cream and the parsley. Season to taste with salt and pepper.

5 **To make the Candied Potatoes** – Put the cooked potatoes in a gratin dish and season with sea salt and pepper. Heat together the butter, garlic, honey, lemon zest and lemon juice, bring to the boil, pour over the potatoes and coat them with the mixture. Place in a preheated oven at 200°C/180°C Fan/Gas 6 and roast until golden all over and sticky. This should take between 25-30 minutes. Stir the potatoes halfway through the cooking time to promote even colouring. Finish the potatoes with the chopped chives or spring onions.

6 **To serve** – slice the gammon thickly, along with a good portion of sauce and a large spoon of potatoes.

Leftover cold gammon is great with salad and pickle, or in a quick sarnie with coarse-grain mustard.

Using up leftovers is so important and they can sometimes end up being better than the original dish. I love leftover gammon in a good sandwich partnered with a nice helping of spiced Piccalilli or, if I have time, I like to add it to a potato gratin, where it almost becomes a meal in itself.

Greek Style Aubergines

A little taste of the Mediterranean sneaking in ahead of the summer months to come.

Ingredients

4 medium-size aubergines

4 tablespoons olive oil

1 large onion, peeled and thinly sliced

1 large garlic clove, chopped and pasted with 1 teaspoon sea salt

½ teaspoon fresh ground black pepper

¼ teaspoon ground cinnamon

1 teaspoon dried oregano

1 tablespoon tomato puree

50ml water or vegetable stock

200g feta cheese

Topping

4 eggs

200ml yoghurt

Salt and pepper for seasoning

1 small lemon

6 black olives

6 stems of parsley, leaves chopped

Serves 4

What you do

1. Preheat the oven grill to high or use a griddle pan.

2. Cut the aubergines in half and then each half into 6 long strips.

3. Brush the strips with some of the olive oil, sprinkle with sea salt and black pepper.

4. Place on a tray under the grill or cook in batches on the griddle.

5. Grill/griddle until golden and soft through – make sure you turn throughout cooking. Drain on kitchen paper.

6. Cook the onion in a little olive oil, sprinkle with a little sea salt and pepper and cook slowly until soft and golden. Add the garlic, cinnamon and oregano and stir

through. Add the tomato puree and water or vegetable stock, stirring to combine. Place a layer of aubergine in the base of a gratin dish, spoon over the onion mixture and crumble the feta cheese over the top, then use the remaining aubergine to create another layer.

7 For the topping, beat together the eggs, yoghurt, salt and pepper and spoon over the top of the aubergine. Finish with thin slices of lemon and the black olives. Bake in a preheated oven at 200°C/180°C Fan/Gas 6 for 30 minutes until golden. Remove and sprinkle with the chopped parsley. Leave to stand for 10 minutes and serve with a simple green salad and crusty bread.

The cooking time for the dish is a guideline as the size of aubergines do vary. The key to success is to make sure that the aubergines are really soft and cooked through, almost wrinkly and golden on top. They are also yummy served cold at room temperature the next day.

Hot Smoked Mackerel with Crisp Pancetta, Rocket and Spring Herb Salad, served with Roasted Garlic Soured Cream

Mackerel, such a beautiful and versatile fish.

Ingredients

4 x 175g-200g mackerel fillets, pin-bones removed

Rub

1 level teaspoon garlic granules

½ level teaspoon dried dill

½ teaspoon sugar

1 level teaspoon sea salt

1 teaspoon pink peppercorns -ground

Zest of 1 small lemon – use the rest to slice, ready to place under the fillets

Salad garnish

4 strips pancetta

1 small bunch spring herbs – parsley, mint, chives, leaves picked

300g mixed leaves

½ small lemon

Sea salt and pepper to season

Soured cream dressing

1 teaspoon creamed horseradish

4 garlic cloves, roasted

1 teaspoon chopped herbs, e.g. chives

200ml soured cream

Serves 4

What you do

1. **To prepare the Mackerel** – Mix the ingredients for the rub together and sprinkle all over the fillets. Lay the slices of lemon on a convection tray, or foil tray with perforations and place the fish on top – this will stop them sticking.

2. **For indoor cooking**, preheat your grill to medium-high heat. **Alternatively, cook outside on your BBQ** – light the BBQ with ½ a chimney of charcoal and set the coals to cook indirect; the temperature should read between 180°C and 200°C.

3 Cook the pancetta strips between 2 sheets of foil and the garlic in a parcel of foil with a teaspoon of olive oil. Place both in the centre of the BBQ grill and cook for 10-15 minutes. Alternatively, place them under the indoor grill to cook for 15-20 minutes, turning them over halfway through the cooking time. The pancetta should be crisp and the garlic soft.

4 **To cook the mackerel on the BBQ** – Add 2 tablespoons of pre-soaked apple or cherry wood chips directly to the coals, place the tray of mackerel in the centre of the BBQ grill, close the lid and smoke for 15 minutes. Remove and rest for 5 minutes.

5 **To cook under an indoor grill** – Place the tray of mackerel under the gill and cook for approximately 7-8 minutes on each side. The skin should crisp up at the edges and the flesh should look creamy in colour.

6 **To assemble** – Mix together the salad and herb leaves, drizzle with a little lemon juice and sprinkle with sea salt and pepper. Set aside.

7 Make the soured cream dressing by mashing the garlic with the horseradish and stirring in the herbs and soured cream.

8 Place a handful of salad on 4 serving plates, add the mackerel next to it, spoon the soured cream next to the fillet, place the pancetta strip at an angle across the 3 elements and serve.

Low ‘n’ Slow Cooked Duck Legs with Pickled Vegetables

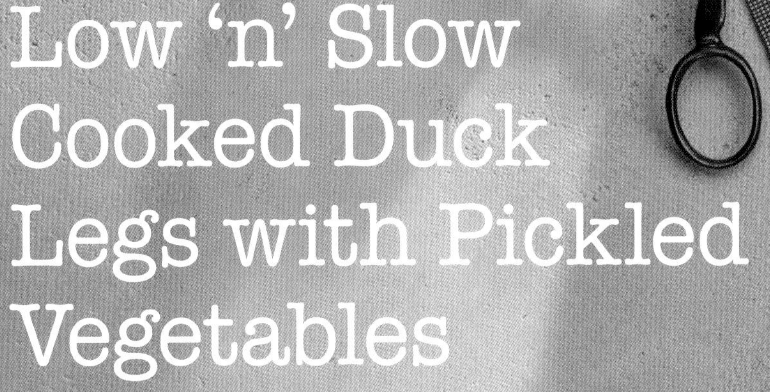

Ingredients

4 duck leg/thigh joints

300ml chicken stock

1 teaspoon sea salt

¼ teaspoon black pepper

2 sprigs of thyme

1 medium bulb of garlic

Brine

100ml white vinegar

500ml water

25g granulated sugar

¼ teaspoon coriander seeds

1 tablespoon sea salt

Salad

500g spring cabbage, kale or broccoli, trimmed and sliced, leaving some leaves whole

300g carrots, peeled and cut into even long lengths

½ small red onion, thinly sliced

Serves 4

What you do

1. Preheat your oven to 160°C/140°C Fan/Gas 3.

2. Pat the duck legs dry all over with kitchen paper, mix the sea salt and black pepper together and sprinkle all over the legs.

3. Place a large non-stick frying pan over a high heat and, once hot, place the legs in the pan and cook until golden all over.

4. Remove the legs from the pan and pop on a plate, then pour in 100ml of the stock and bring to the boil, scraping up any sticky juices with the back of a wooden spoon.

5. Pour the juices into a casserole dish and add the duck and the remaining stock. Cut the garlic bulb in half around the middle, add to the

dish and throw in the thyme. Cover with a lid and cook for 2 hours. In the last 30 minutes of cooking, remove the lid and open roast the duck to re-crisp the skin.

6 Meanwhile, prepare the pickled salad by mixing the brine ingredients in the bottom of a medium bowl, stir to dissolve the salt and sugar. Taste to ensure the balance is good for you, adding more salt or sugar according to your palate. Add the prepared salad vegetables, cover and chill for 2 hours.

7 Once the duck is cooked and crisp, remove the legs and keep warm; they should be tender and falling off the bone. Strain the juices into a pan, simmer and add a little arrowroot or cornflour mixed with water to thicken slightly.

8 Spoon some of the duck sauce onto warmed plates, top with the duck leg and serve with the pickled vegetables.

I love this dish and sometimes serve a little pot of Béarnaise sauce with it. You can make the butter sauce recipe on page 28 and add a dessert spoon each of little capers and chopped gherkin, plus a little chopped tarragon or chervil if you have some. If not, some parsley or chives will be good.

Chinese Duck, Broccoli, Spring Onion and Sesame

A real celebratory dish.

Ingredients

1 x 2.75kg duck fresh or frozen

6 slices of fresh, peeled root ginger

6 spring onions cut in to 3-inch length

Spice rub

2 tablespoons five-spice powder

1 dessertspoon Sichuan peppercorns

1 tablespoon whole black peppercorns

3 tablespoons cumin seeds

1 tablespoon mandarin or orange zest, grated

100g sea salt

To finish

4 tablespoons malt syrup

Salad

450g broccoli, trimmed weight

1 teaspoon of sea salt

12 spring onions , trimmed

1 tablespoon peanut oil

1 teaspoon sesame oil

2 garlic cloves, peeled and thinly sliced

1 teaspoon sesame seeds

1 teaspoon chopped ginger

1 small sliced chilli

2 tablespoons light soy sauce

2 tablespoons mirin rice wine

2 tablespoons lime juice

Serves 4-6

What you do

1 Rinse the duck well under cold water, drain and blot it completely dry with kitchen paper.

2 First, gently roast both peppercorns and cumin seeds in a dry pan for 1 minute until aromatic. Grind to a powder in a mortar and pestle or a spice grinder. Mix this together with all the other ingredients for the spice rub and apply half of it to the inside of the duck and the other half to

the outside. Wrap up well in cling film and place on a plate in the refrigerator for 24 hours.

3 The next day, unwrap the duck and wipe away any of the excess spices from the inside and outside. Place the slices of ginger and the spring onions in the cavity.

4 Preheat the oven to 170°C/150°C Fan/Gas 3.

5 Place the duck in a roasting tray and put it in the oven, checking at 15 minutes intervals to baste and spoon away the rendered fat – this will create a crisp skin. Cook for 1 hour and 50 minutes, then turn the heat up to 200°C/180°C Fan/Gas 6, brush with the malt syrup and roast for another 10-15 minutes until it is really crispy and deep golden. Remove and rest the duck. I switch the oven off and leave the duck inside with the door open.

6 **For the broccoli salad** – Bring a pan of water to the boil and add a teaspoon of salt. Cook the broccoli until just tender, adding the spring onions for 2 minutes at the end of cooking, drain, cover and keep warm. Heat the peanut oil in a wok, add the sesame oil and slithers of garlic and sesame seeds and fry until they just start to colour. Add the chopped ginger and chilli and stir through for 10 seconds, then add the remaining ingredients. Plate the broccoli and spring onions and pour the dressing over the top.

7 To serve the duck, pull away the leg and thigh joint and cut them through at the joint where the thigh meets the leg, to give 4 pieces. Cut along the middle of the breastbone and remove them whole, cutting each into 3. Alternatively, you can shred the whole duck and serve it that way.

8 I love fresh or rice noodles with this dish. Alternatively, if you shred the duck, you can serve in lettuce leaves or the classic little pancakes with shredded cucumber, shredded spring onion and hoisin sauce.

Welsh Lamb Shoulder Stuffed with Farro and Green Olives

In praise of Welsh lamb!

Ingredients

1.5-1.7kg boned shoulder of Welsh lamb

Sea salt and black pepper

For the stuffing

25g butter

1 large onion, peeled and finely chopped

3 large garlic cloves, peeled and grated

300g minced lamb

2 tablespoons preserved lemon, chopped

250g cooked farro or freekeh grain

8 large green olives, roughly chopped

4 anchovies, finely chopped

1 heaped tablespoon sultanas or currants, soaked in white wine for 1 hour

1 tablespoon parsley, chopped

1 tablespoon chopped mint

1 rounded teaspoon sea salt

1 level teaspoon black pepper

1 medium free-range egg

75g breadcrumbs

To finish

1 tablespoon runny honey

The grated zest of a medium lemon

Serves 4-6

What you do

1 **To make the stuffing** – First cook the onion. Melt the butter in a pan, add the onion, 4 tablespoons of water and sauté over a low heat until soft and sticky. Remove and cool slightly. Meanwhile, combine everything else for the stuffing in a mixing bowl, then add the onions; combine and season with sea salt and pepper.

2 Open the lamb out onto your board and season liberally with sea salt and black pepper. Spread the stuffing across the length of the lamb, tie it into a roll with kitchen string and tuck the ends in. This can be done the day before and refrigerated overnight.

3 **To cook** – Preheat the oven to 180°C/160°C Fan/Gas 4.

4 Put the lamb on a roasting tray, cover with foil and roast for 2¼ hours. Remove the foil for the final half hour of cooking, mixing the honey and lemon zest together and brushing over the lamb.

5 Place the lamb in a warm place to rest.

6 For a quick sauce, spoon away any excess fat, deglaze the pan with 100ml white wine and scrape up the sticky juices. Pour in 250ml of chicken stock and a teaspoon of honey. Bubble up for 5 minutes and thicken with 1 rounded teaspoon of cornflour mixed with 4 tablespoons of water. Stir until thickened, it should be syrupy in consistency.

7 Carve the lamb, drizzle with the sauce and serve with some delicious seasonal greens. Alternatively, serve with a delicious hummus with coriander and preserved lemon.

Welsh lamb is such a versatile ingredient and here I have given it a little Mediterranean treatment. It will make a delicious treat for a family gathering at Easter. It is also stunning cooked on the BBQ, using indirect heat at 160°C for about 1 hour 20 minutes. Apply the honey and lemon during the last 15 minutes of cooking.

Hummus with Preserved Lemon

Ingredients

200g dried chickpeas

1½ teaspoons bicarbonate of soda

Additions

6 tablespoons tahini

Zest and juice of 1 large unwaxed lemon, a whole chopped preserved lemon, or more to taste

3 fat garlic cloves, grated

1 small bunch (60g) fresh coriander

1 teaspoon each of fennel and cumin – dry roasted for 30 seconds and then ground together

Sea salt, to taste

Serves 4-6

What you do

1. First, put the chickpeas in a bowl and cover with twice the volume of cold water. Stir in 1 teaspoon of the bicarbonate of soda and leave to soak for 24 hours.

2. Next day, drain the chickpeas, rinse well and put in a large pan. Cover with cold water and add the rest of the bicarbonate of soda.

3. Bring to the boil, then turn down the heat and simmer gently until they are super soft – this can take a while, it all depends on the chickpeas! Add more hot water during cooking if they seem to be boiling dry.

4 Once soft, remove from the heat and leave them to cool in the water. Drain well, reserving the cooking liquid (I chill this for an hour).

5 Place the chickpeas and 200ml of the cooled cooking water in a processor and blend until smooth. Add the other ingredients and keep running the processor whilst you pour in 100ml more of the chilled cooking water. Stop the motor, taste and adjust with sea salt and lemon juice.

Spoon onto a serving plate and ease into a flat circle with the back of a spoon. Garnish with sliced preserved lemon or grated lemon zest, toasted cumin and fennel seeds and some parsley leaves and drizzle with olive oil.

Lamb Cutlets with Dukkah Creamed Feta

Ingredients

12 lamb chops, French-trimmed

12 leaves of mint

60g feta cheese, cut into 12 pieces

6 large pitted green olives, cut in half

Pre-coating

50g plain flour

¼ teaspoon sea salt

125ml cold water to create a thin batter

Dukkah Coating

1 teaspoon cloves

1 teaspoon fennel seeds

1 teaspoon cumin seeds

1 teaspoon coriander seeds

1 level teaspoon turmeric

1 level teaspoon chilli flakes

½ teaspoon of chilli powder

1 heaped tablespoon hazelnuts, finely chopped

1 heaped tablespoon pistachios, finely chopped

1 tablespoon sesame seeds

Serves 4-6

What you do

The spice blend for dukkah is delicious, aromatic, and versatile. You can use it as a dry rub for larger joints, such as shoulder or leg of meat, a whole chicken, or for adding the finishing touch to a simple grilled steak. I also use it to sprinkle over soups and salads, as well as an appetiser with bread and olive oil.

1. To make the dukkah, heat a frying pan and dry roast the cloves, fennel, coriander and cumin until fragrant. Place in a pestle and mortar or a spice grinder and break down to form a coarse powder. Combine the spices with the rest of

the dukkah ingredients in a bowl and mix until well.

2 Cut a pocket into the side of each lamb chop, fill with a mint leaf, piece of feta cheese and half an olive, then press the edges back together.

3 Make the coating batter with the flour, salt and enough water so the spices will stick. Dip each cutlet into the batter and then into the spices to coat. Repeat until all the cutlets are coated.

4 When you are ready to cook them, heat the oven to 200°C/180°C Fan/Gas 6. Place on a baking sheet, brush lightly with olive oil and roast in the oven for 15 minutes for rare, 20 minutes for medium-rare and 25 minutes for medium. Remove from the oven and rest for 5 minutes before serving.

5 Serve with the cauliflower tabbouleh and creamed feta (see pages 96-97) and some green pickled chillies, available from most supermarkets and deli shops.

This is another dish that you can tackle the day before, getting the cutlets stuffed, coated, covered and chilled. I also like to serve them with pickled seasonal vegetables. There are examples to try in this book, such as those with the duck legs and the potted seafood, they eat really well with lamb.

Cauliflower Tabbouleh

Ingredients

½ a large cauliflower, trimmed and cut into florets

1 small bunch parsley, all finely chopped

1 small bunch mint, leaves only, chopped

1 small bunch coriander, all finely chopped

6 radishes, sliced and soaked in 1 tablespoon of white wine vinegar for 10 minutes

4 spring onions, trimmed and thinly sliced

Zest of 1 medium lemon

Dressing

5 tablespoons olive oil

2 tablespoons lemon juice

1 large garlic clove, peeled and grated

1 teaspoon Dijon mustard

1 tablespoon capers

1 level teaspoon sea salt

½ teaspoon ground black pepper

Serves 4

What you do

1. To make the cauliflower grains, place the raw florets into a food processor and pulse until the consistency of couscous is formed.

2. Tip into a large mixing bowl, add all the other ingredients, and toss until well combined.

3. Mix all the ingredients together for the dressing and pour over the tabbouleh. Mix well and serve.

Creamed Feta

Ingredients

250g feta cheese

120ml sour cream or low-fat Greek yoghurt

Zest from 1 medium lemon

1 small garlic clove, peeled and grated

1 tablespoon fresh herbs e.g. parsley and mint, chopped

½ teaspoon sea salt

¼ teaspoon freshly-ground black pepper

To finish

2 tablespoons olive oil

¼ teaspoon chipotle chilli flakes

1 teaspoon dukka mix (see Page 94)

Serves 4

What you do

1. Combine all the ingredients in a food processor or blender and process until smooth. Taste and adjust the seasoning, if necessary.

2. Spoon into a serving bowl and use the back of a small spoon to create a swirl on the surface of the dip. Drizzle with olive oil and sprinkle with the dukka and the chilli flakes.

Spring Chicken

A delicious roast, reminiscent of the classic Chicken Bonne Femme.

Ingredients

2kg free-range chicken

250ml dry white wine

A few garlic cloves, crushed

3 tablespoons olive oil, to drizzle

1 small lemon

750g baby new potatoes

1 bunch spring onions, trimmed

Herb dressing

75ml lemon juice

1 flat teaspoon sea salt

½ black pepper

4 tablespoons spring herbs e.g. chives, thyme leaves, parsley, chervil or tarragon, chopped – a mix of a couple would be good

To finish

400g asparagus, trimmed

2 little gem lettuces, quartered lengthways

Serves 4-6

What you do

1. Heat the oven to 200°C/180°C Fan/Gas 6. Put the chicken in a roasting tin with the wine and garlic, drizzle 3 tablespoons of olive oil over the top and sprinkle with sea salt and pepper. Slice the lemon thinly and arrange over the breast. Roast for 1 hour.

2. Meanwhile, parboil the potatoes for 8 minutes. Drain and steam dry in the hot pan for a few minutes, then squash with the back of a fork. When the chicken has been roasting for 45 minutes, add the potatoes to the tray together with the trimmed spring onions, toss in the pan juices and continue roasting.

3. Make the dressing for the chicken by placing everything in a blender and whizz to form a green coloured liquid. Pour over the chicken after 1 hour of cooking and

continue cooking for 20 minutes. In the last 10 minutes, add the wedges of lettuce and the trimmed asparagus. Remove from the oven, cover with a sheet of foil and rest for 20 minutes.

I sometimes add some chunks of pancetta or thick-cut bacon to the potatoes when they are roasting and pop a pot of wild garlic pesto on the table to dollop on the chicken. It really is delicious.

Green Papaya Salad

Ingredients

50g dried shrimps

50g raw peanuts

450g firm green papaya or 2 green mangoes

3 fat garlic cloves

2 red bird eye chillies, deseeded and chopped

80g Chinese long beans (or use French beans), trimmed and cut into 1½ inch lengths

Dressing

4 tablespoons fish sauce

4 tablespoons lime juice

2 tablespoons palm sugar, grated

12 plum tomatoes, halved

Serves 4-6

What you do

1. First, soak the shrimps in cold water for about 20 minutes.

2. Meanwhile, heat a frying pan, add the peanuts and dry roast them until they turn golden brown, remove and decant into a bowl to cool.

3. Using a wide-head speed peeler, remove the skin from the papaya or mango. Then, using either a mandolin or a peeler, shred the flesh of the fruit. Leave the layer directly surrounding the seeds/stone.

4. Run some cold water into a bowl and soak the papaya to remove some of the sharpness and to crisp it up for about 5 minutes. Drain well on kitchen paper.

5. Put the papaya in a mixing bowl. Drain the shrimp, squeeze out any excess water and roughly chop.

6 Place the chillies and garlic in a large bowl and pound with a pestle or rolling pin to bruise and release the flavours. Add the green beans, shrimps and peanuts and continue pounding until the beans split. The ingredients should be crushed and well mixed.

7 Mix together the fish sauce, lime juice and sugar in a small bowl, stirring until the sugar is dissolved. Drizzle a little at a time into the mixture, stirring to incorporate thoroughly.

8 Now slowly stir in the papaya, lightly pounding between additions. Finally, stir in the tomatoes and serve.

Although tomatoes are not in season at this time of year, I do start to get a yearning for them after the winter months. In this recipe I have used a small plum variety, 'Santa', which have good flavour and are available earlier in the year and perfect for this recipe.

Thai Fishcakes

Thai food is so beautifully aromatic and colourful, with lots of powerful flavour.

Ingredients

450g white fish fillets e.g. ling, haddock, hake or coley, cut into chunks

2 tablespoons Thai fish sauce

2-3 tablespoons red curry paste, depending on how spicy you like it (see page 113)

2 kaffir lime leaves, shredded, or 1 strip lime zest, shredded finely

1 tablespoon fresh coriander, chopped

1 large egg, beaten

1 teaspoon palm or muscovado sugar

1 level teaspoon sea salt

75g French beans, ends trimmed and sliced into thin rounds

250ml sunflower oil, for frying

Sweet and Sour Dipping Sauce

Make sure your veggies are super finely diced like little gems

50ml white wine vinegar

30g caster sugar

2 tablespoons water

1 tablespoon Thai fish sauce

40g cucumber, very finely diced

40g carrot, very finely diced

30g onion, very finely diced

2 red bird eye chillies, thinly sliced

Serves 4-6

What you do

1. First, make the sauce by mixing together the vinegar, sugar and water in a small bowl until the sugar has dissolved. Stir in the fish sauce, cucumber, carrot, onion and chillies. Cover and chill until ready to serve. Spoon into small pots for dipping and set aside.

2. **To make the fish cakes** – Put the fish chunks into a food processor and pulse until broken down and

combined to a paste. Decant into a mixing bowl, add the fish sauce, curry paste, kaffir lime/zest, coriander, egg, sugar and salt into a mixing bowl. Wet your hand and whip together vigorously to compact the mixture, it will become almost like smooth jelly. Stir in the beans.

3 Divide the mixture into 16 portions, roll each portion into a ball, then flatten into a thin disc. These should be rustic to look at, not perfect rounds. Place on a plate and cover with cling film and refrigerate until ready to cook.

4 **To cook** – Heat the oil in a large pan and fry the fishcakes in batches for 1 minute each side – they should be golden brown. Drain on kitchen paper and keep warm until all the fishcakes are cooked.

5 Serve with the dipping sauce. I also like a shredded salad of cucumber, carrot and onion with this; it also makes a nice garnish.

These are usually served as an appetizer, but they can easily be turned into a main meal with the addition of a salad – green papaya is perfect. Serve with a little bed of rice and dipping sauce and you have a fabulous plate of food.

Red Pork Curry

Time to get physical with your mortar and pestle and make this delicious, complex dish.

Ingredients

1 tablespoon sunflower oil

2 rounded tablespoons Thai red curry paste (see page 113)

5cm piece fresh root ginger, peeled and finely chopped

3 large garlic cloves, peeled and grated

1 rounded teaspoon turmeric

750g lean pork – loin or tenderloin – cut into thin strips

300ml chicken stock, fresh or from a jelly stock concentrate

1 flat dessertspoon light muscovado sugar

2 tablespoons Thai fish Sauce

4 kaffir lime leaves, or zest and juice of 1 lime

300g green beans, trimmed and cut in half

300ml coconut cream

1 small pack fresh Thai basil, stalks removed

Serves 4

What you do

1. Put a wok or chef pan over a high heat and let it get really hot. Add the sunflower oil and the curry paste, stir into the oil and cook for 30 seconds. Stir in the ginger and garlic and fry for 1 minute. Stir in the turmeric (add a splash of the stock if anything starts to stick, this will dissolve any stickiness away before it burns), add the pork and stir through the paste to coat.

2. Pour in the stock, sugar, fish sauce and lime leaves or zest and juice. Bring to the boil, then cover and simmer gently over a very low heat for 20 minutes, until the pork is tender and cooked through. Taste and season if necessary.

3. Add the beans and coconut cream in the last 10 minutes of cooking time. Stir in the basil leaves and serve with fragrant Thai rice.

Thai Red Curry Paste

Ingredients

2 teaspoons each cumin and coriander seeds

5 red bird's eye chillies, roughly chopped

2 tablespoons paprika

3 lemongrass stalks, roughly chopped

4cm piece fresh galangal or ginger, chopped

8 fresh kaffir lime leaves or the finely grated zest of 2 limes

2 shallots, chopped

5 large garlic cloves, chopped

Stalks from 80g bunch fresh coriander

1 heaped teaspoon shrimp paste

3 tablespoons fish sauce

2 tablespoons sunflower oil

What you do

1. Heat a small pan and dry roast the cumin and coriander seeds until aromatic – about 30 seconds. Pour into a pestle and mortar or a spice blender and grind to a powder.

2. Place everything in a food processor and blend to form a smooth paste.

Vanilla Custard Tart with Caramelised Blood Oranges

Ingredients

Oranges in Caramel

4 blood or regular oranges

150g sugar

150ml water

Pastry cases

4 sheets fillo pastry

75g unsalted butter, melted

Custard

6 large (60g) egg yolks

125g tablespoons granulated sugar

30g plain flour

30g cornstarch

400ml whole milk

200ml double cream

½ vanilla bean, split and seeded, or 1 teaspoon vanilla paste

Makes 4

What you do

1. First, make the oranges in caramel. Use a knife or a wide-head peeler to remove the very outside skin from two of the oranges and cut into very fine strips. Using a serrated knife, cut the skin and pith from all the oranges, cut into slices and place in a heat proof bowl.

2. Put the sugar with half the water in a small pan and stir over a medium heat until the sugar dissolves. Leave the pan to simmer gently and do not stir, until the sugar turns a deep caramel.

3. Carefully hold the pan over the sink at arm's length, as there will be some spluttering, and pour in the rest of the water, stir to dissolve any lumps of caramel.

4. Pour three-quarters of the caramel over the orange slices. Put the remaining caramel back on the heat and add the orange zest strips. Simmer for 5 minutes then pour over the oranges.

5 **Bake the fillo pastry cases** – Lay 3 sheets of fillo on top of each other and cut into 4 large squares. The squares should be large enough to fit the mould and rise above the edge slightly like a pointed handkerchief. Brush 4 large muffin tins with some of the melted butter. Brush 4 squares of fillo with butter and line the cases, butter side up. Repeat this with the remaining fillo squares, positioning them so that they create points all the way around; push them into place so they line the moulds neatly. Bake in a preheated oven at 190°C/170°C Fan/Gas 5 for 15-20 minutes; the pastry cases should be firm and lightly golden. Remove and cool.

6 **To make the custard cream filling** – Whisk together the egg yolks and sugar just until pale yellow and creamy, then whisk in the cornstarch and flour and set aside.

7 In a medium saucepan, heat the milk, cream, vanilla pod and seeds or vanilla paste, over a medium heat until it almost reaches boiling point. If using a vanilla pod, remove it at this stage. Gradually pour the hot milk over the eggs and sugar mixture, whisking constantly to combine.

8 Pour into a clean pan and cook over a low-medium heat, stirring constantly, until the custard is formed and thickened. Do not boil, as the eggs will curdle. Pour into a heat proof bowl and place a sheet of non-PVC film/disc of parchment paper directly onto the surface of the custard to prevent a skin forming as it cools. Let it cool to room temperature, then refrigerate until chilled.

9 **To assemble** – Remove the fillo tart cases from the tins and place on serving plates. Whisk up the custard a little (make sure it is room temperature) and spoon into the cases. Top with a couple of slices of orange, the zest and caramel, serving the remaining oranges in a dish at the table.

Rhubarb and Orange Pudding

Rhubarb! Rhubarb! Rhubarb!

Ingredients

Serves 4-6

Rhubarb filling

600g rhubarb (trimmed weight), cut into 2-3cm lengths

125g light Muscovado sugar

1 teaspoon ginger, chopped

1 teaspoon orange zest

Sponge

200g golden caster sugar

225g unsalted butter, softened and diced

200g self-raising flour, sifted

Zest of 1 large orange

100ml fresh orange juice (use the one you zested)

4 medium free-range eggs

1 teaspoon vanilla extract

Topping

40g slivered almonds

1 tablespoon demerara sugar

What you do

1. Preheat the oven to 200°C/180°C Fan/Gas 6.

2. **To make the fruit base** – Put the rhubarb, sugar, ginger and orange zest into a bowl and mix together briefly. Butter a 2L gratin style dish, put the rhubarb mixture in the bottom and spread evenly.

3. **For the topping** – Mix the almonds with 2 level tablespoons of the caster sugar and set aside.

4. **To make the sponge** – Place all the sponge ingredients in the bowl of a food processor and cream together, or into a bowl and use an electric whisk to combine. Spoon the mixture over the rhubarb and spread evenly with the back of a warmed spoon. Sprinkle the top with the almonds and sugar. Bake in the oven for about 1 hour or until a

skewer inserted at the centre comes out clean.

I love to serve this dessert warm with a dollop of Greek style yoghurt.

Queen of Puddings with Lemon and Elderflower Curd

Ingredients

Custard

400ml whole milk

200ml double cream

1 medium lemon, zest only

25g butter (extra to butter ramekins)

4 large (60g) eggs yolks (save whites for meringue)

100g caster sugar

4 x 5cm thick slices of brioche

Topping

140g good lemon curd

2 tablespoons elderflower cordial

Meringue

225g caster sugar

The 4 saved egg whites

Serves 4

What you do

1. Butter 4 large individual ramekins or chef rings (place on a baking sheet lined with parchment) and heat the oven to 180°C/160°C Fan/Gas 4.

2. Bring the milk, cream, zest of 1 lemon and 25g butter to the boil, then turn off the heat.

3. Beat the 4 egg yolks with the 100g caster sugar, then strain the hot milk over them, whisking constantly to make a custard.

4. Push the brioche slices into the ramekins or the base of the chef rings, pour in the custard and let them sit to soak for 5 minutes, then bake for 20 minutes.

5. When the brioche has 6 minutes left in the oven, spread the sugar for the meringue onto a parchment-lined baking sheet and heat in the oven (the same temperature) for 6 minutes. Remove the brioche

bases and the sugar. Whisk the 4 egg whites until they form peaks, then whisk in the hot sugar and continue whisking for a couple of minutes, until the meringue is thick and glossy. Mix the lemon curd with the elderflower cordial and spoon onto the brioche bases. Next, spoon the meringue into a piping bag fitted with a star nozzle, then pipe a 'Mr. Whippy' style meringue topping.

6 Finish the meringue tops by caramelising the outside with a Chef's blowtorch. If you don't have one, pop into a preheated oven at 220°C/200°C Fan/Gas 7 for about 7 minutes until they start to colour. If using chef rings, to decant, run a knife around the inside of each ring to release the pudding. Use a spatula to ease onto a serving plate.

7 Serve with a scoop of vanilla ice cream – utter bliss!

If you do not have a blowtorch, set your oven to 220°C/200°C Fan/Gas 7 and bake for 7 minutes.

Sunday Crumble

Ingredients

Fruit filling

25g unsalted butter

3 medium pears or apples, peeled, cored and quartered

600g rhubarb, trimmed and cut into chunks

2 pieces of preserved ginger, chopped

1 tablespoon ginger wine (optional), or use orange juice

3 tablespoons light muscovado sugar

1 level teaspoon vanilla paste or extract

1 heaped teaspoon orange zest, grated

1 teaspoon cornflour

Crumble Topping

75g pan-roasted almonds or hazelnuts

25g porridge oats

75g unsalted butter, cut into small cubes

125g self raising flour

1 teaspoon orange zest

50g light muscovado sugar

25g demerara sugar

To finish

6 half teaspoons (blobs) of set honey

Serves 6-8

What you do

1. Melt the butter in a pan, add the pears, rhubarb, ginger, ginger wine/ orange juice, sugar, vanilla, orange zest and cornflour. Cook over a low heat for about 10-12 minutes until the fruit is tender but not falling apart. Transfer the fruit into a large buttered ovenproof dish and set aside.

2. Heat your oven to 200°C/Fan 180°C/Gas 6.

3. To make the crumble topping, tip all the ingredients into a food processor and pulse to form largish crumbs. Sprinkle the topping over

the fruit, stud with the honey blobs and bake for 30-35 minutes until golden brown on top.

4 Serve with custard, ice cream, crème fraîche, cream or Greek yoghurt.

The rhubarb season arches from December to September, starting with force grown and then field grown, so this crumble will serve you well throughout. My lovely mum, Betty, would always add a couple of handfuls of new season strawberries to a rhubarb crumble or pie. A real celebration where seasons meet.

The Welsh Collection

Let's Celebrate!

The Welsh food scene has come a long way in the last 20 years. For 10 years I ran a consultancy that helped showcase Welsh food, food producers and Wales as a great tourism destination to everyone, through a series of events and festivals around the world. The pinnacle of this came in 2009 at the annual Smithsonian Folklife Festival in Washington DC, when more than 160 participants took part in a 10-day event sharing their knowledge, talent, skills and expertise.

Food certainly played a central role. I worked on the idea of a 'Presentation Theatre' where we could share a mixture of storytelling and cooking. The amazing team of chefs who accompanied me included Hazel Thomas, who was my co-pilot on this project and has become a very special friend; Gareth Johns from Mid Wales, Anthony Evans from Camarthen, Geraldine Trotman from Cardiff Bay (formerly Tiger Bay) and Anna Rees, who came all the way from her tea room in Patagonia. All of them painted a very colourful picture of life past and present, using a range of traditional recipes, cooking methods, ingredients and anecdotes. We had a wonderful backdrop consisting of a giant Welsh dresser, built from recycled plastic and stocked with items to portray a family museum of collectables in china, literature and photographs. I had asked for raised beds to be planted either side of the stage with a mix of vegetables, herbs and salads to convey the importance of homegrown seasonal ingredients and to show how this tradition still prevails today.

The American audiences took us to their hearts and were really taken by our passion and love of our craft. Groups of people reappeared every day, scribbling down recipes and joining in the fun and laughter. I also had the honour of hosting two afternoon tea parties at the British Embassy where I talked about Welsh food culture and shared many personal anecdotes from my career. As the guests enjoyed a traditional Welsh afternoon tea, I was struck by their genuine interest and appreciation.

As part of the festival, I also worked with a team in the USA to cater for the 1.2 million expected visitors. We created a Welsh pub serving Tomos Watkin ales, along with a fast food-style outlet on the Mall serving up some traditional classics. The catering team handmade more than 70,000 Glamorgan sausages, thousands of bowls of cawl (10,000 kg of lamb were used in total), and endless Welsh cheese platters, with thanks to Abergavenny Fine Foods, and Penderyn Whisky ice cream sundaes.

The experiences from the Smithsonian brought a realisation of just how special our food culture is; how important it is to preserve our food heritage and celebrate the wonderful food scene we have today.

Classic traditional recipes from the Welsh kitchen are like most good dishes, in that they are born out of the simple cooking of local and seasonal ingredients. It is the basis of what clever chefs use to twist into a fine dining piece of art that will look beautiful, but still maintain its roots.

Here are some of my personal favourites that are well travelled and have been very well received. I hope you enjoy them too.

PONT GâR
cosyn
brefu
BACH
THE ABERGAVENNY CREAMERY
WITH BLUEBERRY PIECES
1.5kg℮
THE ABERGAVENNY CREAMERY
CASTLE MEADOWS
CRANBERRY
WITH CRANBERRY PIECES
CAWS CAERFFILI
THE ABERGAVENNY CREAMERY
TINTERN
CHEDDAR CHEESE
WITH ONIONS, CHIVES AND SHALLOTS
1.5kg℮
THE ABERGAVENNY CREAMERY
MUSTARD AND ALE

Glamorgan Sausages

The organisers of the Smithsonian Folklife Festival wanted to call our beloved Glamorgan sausage a cheesedog so that the Americans could relate to it. I said that whilst the Welsh were in town, they had to be Glamorgan Sausages as they were part of our food tradition heritage. 70,000 were sold, so I guess the Americans understood just fine!

Ingredients

25g butter

1 medium-size leek, trimmed, washed and finely chopped

400g fresh breadcrumbs

200g mature Welsh cheddar-type cheese, grated

1 medium-size free-range egg, beaten

1 teaspoon Dijon mustard

¼–½ teaspoon of cayenne pepper

1 tablespoon chopped parsley

Coating

1 heaped tablespoon of flour mixed with 150ml water

200g Panko or fresh-dried breadcrumbs

Sunflower oil for frying

Serves 4

What you do

1. Melt the butter in a frying pan, add the chopped leek and sauté until just soft. Spoon into a mixing bowl, spread out and cool slightly.

2. Add the breadcrumbs and cheese to the bowl. Mix the egg with the mustard and cayenne pepper in a small bowl and pour into the mixture, adding the parsley. Mix together and divide into 8 portions, squeeze and shape into even sausage shapes.

3. **To coat the sausages** – Whisk together the flour and water in a medium-sized mixing bowl; it should look like single cream consistency. Spread the breadcrumbs on a small plate. Dip the sausages one at a time, coating them with the batter, then roll through the breadcrumbs, making sure the ends are also coated.

4 **To cook** – Heat a large frying pan and add 1cm of sunflower oil, testing its readiness with a couple of breadcrumbs; they should sizzle gently. Fry the sausages (in 2 batches if your pan is not large enough), turning occasionally so they are golden all over. Drain well on kitchen paper.

5 Serve with a fruit chutney or onion marmalade and shredded seasonal salad.

I have made thousands of these with my team over the years to serve at events celebrating Welsh culture around the world. Small versions of these can be made, frozen on trays and then bagged up the next day. To cook straight from frozen, just add an additional 5 minutes to the cooking time. People love them, so make plenty.

Laverbread, Cockle and Bacon Cakes with Parsley Salad

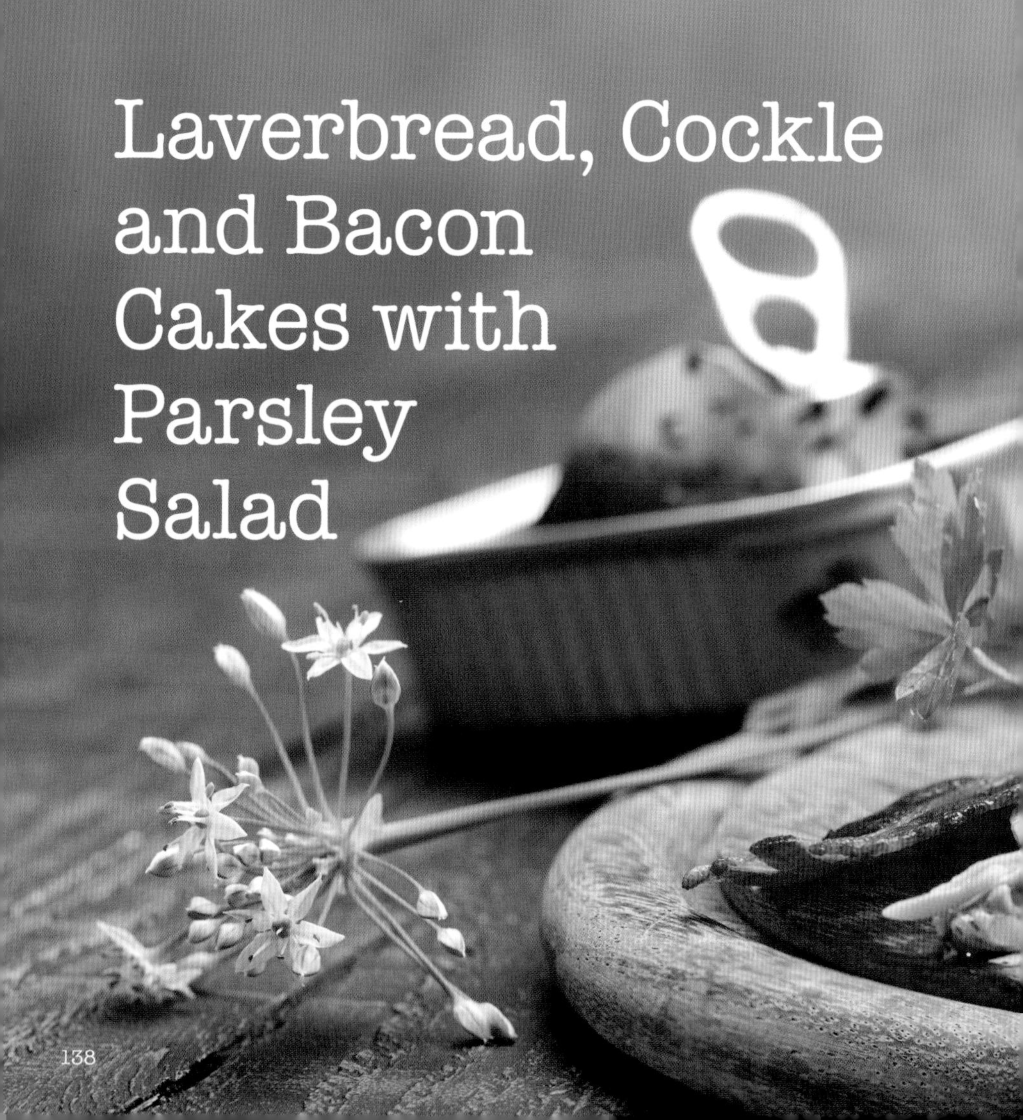

Laver

Laver is such an amazing ingredient, packed full of goodness from the sea. It is commonly known as laverbread, due to the oatmeal it would have been mixed with traditionally before cooking. You can still buy it with added oatmeal, and a tub of fresh cooked cockles at the wonderful indoor market in Swansea. It's culinary history stems from the days when it was served up as part of a full breakfast, particularly in south-west Wales among the mining communities. Thick slices of very fatty bacon would have been fried, and the fat from this would then be used to fry eggs, laverbread, and a sprinkling of cockles. This was a high-energy meal, giving necessary sustenance for what would have been a long and gruelling day underground. These days the application of laverbread in cooking is a little more sophisticated.

Ingredients

The laver cakes

150g Laverbread

Approximately 75g of toasted oats (dry-roasted in a pan for 5 minutes)

1 tablespoon parsley, chopped

50g fresh cockles

½ teaspoon lemon zest

1-2 tablespoons of lemon juice

1 small garlic clove, grated

2 crisply cooked slices of bacon, finely chopped

¼ teaspoon of black pepper

Butter for frying

Salad and dressing

12 stems of parsley, torn

4 crisply-cooked slices of streaky bacon

50g fresh cockles

2 tablespoons lemon juice

4 tablespoons rapeseed or sunflower oil

A couple of twists of black pepper

Serves 4

What you do

1 Place all the ingredients for the laver cakes in a mixing bowl and combine. Set aside for 5 minutes to allow the oats to absorb the moisture. If after this time the mixture is a little wet, add some more oats to firm it up so you can shape it into little cakes for frying.

2 Divide the mixture into 8 portions and shape into little cakes.

3 Heat a large frying pan, add a good walnut-sized piece of butter, wait until it starts to foam, then add the laver and cockle cakes. Cook in batches so you don't overcrowd the pan. Make sure the heat is not too high, as the butter will burn.

4 Allow the cakes to form a crispy crust underneath before turning over. Remove and drain on kitchen paper.

5 Make the salad by tearing the parsley leaves into a bowl. Break up the bacon into pieces and add to the parsley. Spoon in the cockles and add the lemon juice, oil and black pepper. Mix briefly and serve a mound with 2 warm laver cakes per person.

Laver is commonly known as laverbread, due to the oatmeal it would have been mixed with traditionally before cooking.

Cawl

Ingredients

Broth

1kg lamb shank

200g piece of bacon

2 medium leeks, rinsed and chopped

2-3 carrots, scraped and thickly sliced

1-2 turnips, peeled and thickly sliced

1 parsnip, peeled and thickly sliced

1.5 L water

6 Peppercorns

Bay leaf

2 sprigs thyme

To serve

600g lamb loin, trimmed

Sea salt, black pepper

2 sprigs thyme

25g butter

12 small new potatoes, scrubbed and halved

8 small carrots, scrubbed and trimmed

6 small leeks or 2 leeks, chunkily cut

Large handful spring greens, or cabbage

To finish

Parsley, finely chopped

3 stems mint chopped

¼ teaspoon lemon zest

Serves 4

What you do

1 **Prepare the broth** – Wipe the shank with kitchen paper. Place in a large pan with the bacon, chopped vegetables, peppercorns, thyme and bay leaf. Pour in the water and bring to the boil, skimming away any scum that forms on the top. Reduce the heat and simmer gently for 2 hours. The meat should be soft and the broth full of flavour. Remove the meat and vegetables and enjoy these as a fabulous supper with crusty bread. Leave the broth to cool and pop in the fridge over night.

2 The next day or the day after, skim off the fat; I use it for frying little bread slices to serve on the side of the cawl. Tip the stock into a pan and bring to the boil, reduce the heat until low and pop a lid on while you prepare the lamb loin and vegetables.

3 Season the loin with sea salt and black pepper. Heat a large frying pan, add the butter and, when foaming, add the loin and the sprigs of thyme. Bathe the lamb in the butter as it sears and browns all over, this should take about 8 minutes. Preheat the oven to 220°C/200°C Fan/Gas 7. Remove the seared loin and roast in the oven for 10 minutes. Remove and rest for 5 minutes before slicing.

4 Meanwhile, cook the carrot and potatoes until soft, adding the greens and leeks in the last 5 minutes of cooking. Drain well.

5 **To assemble** – Carve the loin into 16 slices and place some vegetables in the base of 4 warmed soup plates. Top with 4 slices of lamb and pour in the lamb broth. Mix the chopped parsley, mint and lemon zest together and sprinkle over the top.

I also love this dish served with a zesty salsa verde. Mix 3 heaped tablespoons of chopped soft herbs, including mint and parsley, add 1 grated clove of garlic, 1 teaspoon lemon zest, 2 tablespoons lemon juice, a tablespoon of capers and 2 chopped anchovies. Mix, season to taste and then stir in enough olive oil to loosen the mixture.

Faggots, Onion Gravy and Mushy Peas

This recipe is a little more refined compared to the ones we made growing up.

Ingredients

Faggots

10 slices thick-cut streaky bacon, finely chopped

1 tablespoon sage, finely chopped

2 teaspoons thyme, finely chopped

1 small yellow onion, finely chopped

Kosher salt and freshly ground black pepper, to taste

450g minced pork

100g pig's liver, finely chopped

360g fresh breadcrumbs

120ml full-fat milk

1/4 teaspoon nutmeg, freshly grated

120ml dry white wine

120ml chicken stock

Onion gravy

4 tablespoons unsalted butter

1 large onion, peeled and thinly sliced

1 tablespoon plain flour

400ml cooking juices from the faggots

75ml Madeira or medium sherry

½ teaspoon Worcestershire sauce

Sea salt and black pepper

Serves 4

What you do

1. **Prepare the faggots** – Preheat your oven to 180°C/160°C Fan/Gas 4. Heat a heavy based pan and add the chopped bacon and cook over a medium heat until the fat is rendered/melted away and the bacon is slightly crisp about 4-6 minutes. Add in the sage, thyme, onion, salt, and pepper; cook, stirring occasionally, until soft and lightly golden, about 7-9 minutes. Tip into a mixing bowl and leave to cool.

2. Take a large mixing bowl and add the pork, liver, bread crumbs, milk, nutmeg, salt, and pepper, spoon in the bacon and onion mixture; mix well to combine.

3. Form mixture into 12 equal balls, with wet hands, roll and smooth them into shape and place in a buttered baking dish. Add the wine and chicken stock and bake, basting occasionally with pan juices, until cooked through, about 25 minutes. Pour off the stock and reserve.

4. To make the onion gravy, melt the butter in a saucepan over medium-low heat; add onion and cook slowly over a low heat, stirring occasionally, until golden brown. This will take between 30-40 minutes. Stir in the flour and cook briefly for 2 minutes.

5. Gradually stir in the reserved stock from the faggots, along with the Madeira/sherry. Bring to the boil and season with the Worcestershire sauce, sea salt and pepper. Lower to a simmer and add the faggots to the gravy with any juices, bubble gently for about 15 minutes while you cook the peas and mash your potatoes.

6. **For mushy peas** – It is a tin of marrowfat peas, heated with 25g butter, a few twists of black pepper and 1 tablespoon crème fraiche. Bubble together gently for 10 minutes and then lightly mash. Stir in a dessertspoon of fresh, chopped mint and serve with the faggots.

7. **For mashed potatoes** – To 600g of cooked mashed potato add 50g butter, sea salt and white pepper to taste, along with 8 scrapes of nutmeg and 2 tablespoons of crème fraiche.

I have served these as a canapé many times for celebrating Wales at events. Little cocktail versions on a stick, topped with a marrowfat pea and a crisp sage leaf – really delicious.

Welsh Rarebit

Ingredients

200ml milk

1½ teaspoons English mustard powder

½ teaspoon cayenne pepper

40g butter

350g mature cheddar-style cheese, grated

A little Worcestershire sauce to taste, if desired

1½ tablespoons plain flour

2 eggs, beaten

4 thick slices of good bread

Serves 4

What you do

1 Pour the milk into a small pan, adding the mustard powder, cayenne pepper and butter. Heat gently, until the butter has melted.

2 Add the cheese and stir to melt, but do not let the mixture boil. Once smooth, taste for seasoning, adding a little Worcestershire sauce if you wish. Stir in the flour and whisk to combine and avoid lumps. Remove from the heat and whisk in the eggs. Leave to cool until just slightly warm; it will thicken as it cools.

3 Preheat your grill to medium-high and toast the bread on both sides. Spoon a good dollop of the rarebit onto the toast, spread thickly and cook until bubbling and golden. Serve immediately.

Note: You can store the rarebit in a container or jar and keep in the fridge for up to 4 days. It can be moulded to sit on top of a fish fillet, such as cod or hake, or on top of a classic beef fillet once it has been seared – finish under the grill.

Welsh Cakes

Ingredients

225g self-raising flour, sieved

110g unsalted butter, plus extra for greasing

1 large free-range egg, beaten

1 tablespoon of currants or raisins

A little milk, if needed

85g golden caster sugar, extra for sprinkling

Makes 24

What you do

1 Rub the butter into the flour until it looks like fine breadcrumbs. Add the sugar and dried fruit and then the egg. Mix to combine and then push together to form a dough. If the mixture feels a little dry, add a little milk.

2 Lightly flour your work surface. Roll out the dough until it is about 5mm/¼ inch thick. Cut into rounds with a 10cm/3-4-inch fluted cutter.

3 Rub a bakestone or a heavy-based pan with a little unsalted butter. Place over a low-medium heat and cook the Welsh cakes slowly until golden underneath and slightly puffed. Turn them over and cook the other side until golden. They will need about 2-3 minutes each side.

4 Remove from the pan and dust with caster sugar while still warm.

Additional yummy things to add to the dough.

Try:

- 1 teaspoon lemon or orange zest, finely grated
- 1 teaspoon vanilla salt (Anglesey Sea Salt Co)
- 1 tablespoon chocolate chips with orange or lemon zest
- 1 tablespoon dried sour cherries or cranberries

Seasonal ingredients

Just look at this list for inspiration!

Vegetables

Purple sprouting, broccoli, cabbages, leeks, curly kale, sea kale, watercress, morel mushrooms, spring greens, sorrel, spring onions, radishes, cauliflower, celeriac, chicory, parsley, mint, potatoes, Jersey Royal new potatoes, rocket, sorrel, artichokes, aubergines, fennel, mangetout, samphire, british asparagus.

Fruits

Pomegranates, rhubarb, blood oranges.

Meat and Game

Hare, wood pigeon, spring lamb, duck.

Seafood

Wild salmon, sea trout, crab, oysters, cockles, cod, hake, John Dory, lemon sole, sea bass, herring, mackerel.

Spring Celebrations

March – St. David's Day
Easter
Mother's Day
Queens Birthday
St Georges Day

About Angela Gray

Angela opened the Cookery School at Llanerch Vineyard in 2011. The School also hosts a number of special events where Angela cooks, chats enthusiastically and promotes the good life through cooking and eating together.

Everything that precedes her time at the School has given her the wealth of experience and knowledge needed to head such an ambitious project. She worked prolifically in the food world, starting her career as a personal chef working in Europe and North America. Her clients included an esteemed list, from European aristocracy to high-profile clients such as Lord Lloyd Webber. Angela took to the helm at a number of restaurants, where she developed her relaxed style of cuisine with a strong Mediterranean influence.

She returned home to Wales, where her career path changed when she attended university in Cardiff and gained a BSc Honours degree in Food Science. Whilst studying, Angela also ran a small catering business and held a twice-monthly Cooking Club from her home. This would later form the basis of two prime time cookery series for BBC Wales, *Hot Stuff* and *More Hot Stuff*. Next came several series for radio, including *My Life on a Plate* and *Packed Lunch*. She still loves to get involved in media projects, but her main focus these days is at the School and writing her cookery books.

At the close of 2016 the School was listed in the top 10 Cookery Schools in *The Independent*, *The Telegraph*, *Sunday Times* and *Evening Standard*. Most recently it was also chosen for the prestigious *National Cookery School Guide*. In Angela's own words, that's the result of teamwork at its best.

Dedication

In memory of my mum Betty, all these books have been a collection of memories and she has been there with me throughout them all.

I would like to thank Huw Jones for his masterful touch in creating all the beautiful images for the books, you are such a talent.

Finally, to Pamela, who I met some years ago when she attended a cookery course at my School. Who knew that she would become a dear friend and my right hand, working tirelessly in helping me make the School a great success. Thank you so very much, Pam.

People we love

- Castle Dairies
  www.castledairies.co.uk
- Halen Môn Sea Salt Co
  www.halenmon.com
- Welsh Lamb and Beef (HCC)
  penylanpantry.com
- Pen Y Lan Pantry/Cheese Pantry
  penylanpantry.com
- One Mile Bakery Cardiff
  www.onemilebakery.com/cardiff
- Ashton Fishmongers
  www.ashtonfishmongers.co.uk
- Wally's Delicatessen
  www.wallysdeli.co.uk
- Dyfi Dystillery
  www.dyfidistillery.com
- Madhav Stores
  59 Lower Cathedral Rd,
  Cardiff CF11 6LW
  (Indian food store and café)
- Eastern Chinese Supermarket
  26 Tudor St, Cardiff CF11 6AH

Metric and imperial equivalents

Weights	Solid
15g	½oz
25g	1oz
40g	1½oz
50g	1¾oz
75g	2¾oz
100g	3½oz
125g	4½oz
150g	5½oz
175g	6oz
200g	7oz
250g	9oz
300g	10½oz
400g	14oz
500g	1lb 2oz
1kg	2lb 4oz
1.5kg	3lb 5oz
2kg	4lb 8oz
3kg	6lb 8oz

Volume	Liquid
15ml	½ floz
30ml	1 floz
50ml	2 floz
100ml	3½ floz
125ml	4 floz
150ml	5 floz (¼ pint)
200ml	7 floz
250ml	9 floz
300ml	10 floz (½ pint)
400ml	14 floz
450ml	16 floz
500ml	18 floz
600ml	1 pint (20 floz)
1 litre	1¾ pints
1.2 litre	2 pints
1.5 litre	2¾ pints
2 litres	3½ pints
3 litres	5¼ pints

Angela's Cookbooks

Angela's cookbooks bring together a collection of recipes inspired by the seasons, her childhood, travels and career in food. They also form the basis of many of the courses run at her Cookery School at Llanerch Vineyard in the Vale of Glamorgan.

Winter Recipes

Everything naturally warms up in colour and flavour in this recipe collection. Angela uses a wide range of ingredients to invigorate the palate, from aromatic spice blends to the punchy flavours of pomegranate molasses, porcini and truffle.

Spring Recipes

Expect fresh, zesty flavours, vibrant colours and lots of inspiring ways to enhance your day-to-day cooking at home.

Summer Recipes

This book features a rich collection of recipes from Angela's travels and her time spent working in the South of France. Barbecuing, dining al fresco, entertaining friends, it's all here.

Autumn Recipes

Colours and flavours become richer and deeper in this book and recipes embrace the wonderful harvest of seasonal ingredients. Angela shares easy ways to entertain so you can be the host with the most.

Festive Recipes

The highlight of the Cookery School calendar is the 'Festive Kitchen' event, where Angela demonstrates a range of inspirational recipes that are all showstoppers, guaranteed to 'wow' friends and family throughout the Christmas and New Year celebrations. This is her very special collection of those recipes.

‘I love this time of year, when we witness nature bursting with new life and with it comes a lovely fresh larder from which we can create lighter and brighter dishes to energise the body and soul. I will, as usual, be encouraging readers to try something new, such as fish tagine, and pushing their culinary skills in making handmade pasta with wild garlic pesto.’